A Figure on the Move

books of poetry by the same author

Between Something and Something
Shape Enduring Mind
A Different Lens
Towards the Mystery

A Figure on the Move

Alastair Macdonald

Breakwater
100 Water Street
P.O. Box 2188
St. John's, Newfoundland A1C 6E6

Illustrations throughout this book by the author.

The Publisher gratefully acknowledges the financial support of the Cultural Affairs Division of the Department of Municipal and Provincial Affairs, Government of Newfoundland and Labrador, and of The Canada Council which has helped make this publication possible.

In this collection, 'The Garden Seat' and 'Passes' are republished, with permission, from Green's Magazine (Canada). Certain other poems included appeared first in Daybreak (Canada), Lines Review (U.K.), The Newfoundland Quarterly (Canada), Oracle (Canada), TickleAce (Canada). Acknowledgements and grateful thanks are here given to all these publications.

Author's photo by Margaret Miles-Cadman

Canadian Cataloguing in Publication Data

Macdonald, Alastair.
   A figure on the move
   Poems.
   ISBN 1-55081-010-3

I. Title.
PS8575.D66F53 1991   C811'.54   C91-097545-0
PR9199.3.M32F53 1991

PRINTED IN CANADA.
10 9 8 7 6 5 4 3 2 1

Contents

The years are long to be
a figure on the move
like these, free, unrestrained
it seems,
in landscapes by oneself,
to drive far off, towards conflict,
tread down fields of time.

The Garden Seat

Back Again

We walk the streets,
pretending nothing strange
is happening, no time
has intervened (and so it seems),
self-consciously as if on eggs,
imagine everyone we meet
is thinking oh that's so and so
back after all those years away
in the job—what was it?—he was in
abroad. Can it have been
so long? How old
he looks. In the park, only
some little children play, rattle
the chains of the swings,
squeal down the chutes.
With trundled babies
child-bride (surely?) housewives shop.
Assaulting blasts of pop buffet
the ears from wide-flung doors of cars
before they're killed with engines cut.
Metal slams as the men park,
and enter offices and banks.
Young strangers all.

The streets and alleys, then,
outran our sight with nods and lures
of the promised what-would-be
in far off regions,
other pictures, casts of life
one had to know.
These fields were Italy and France,
this part of town America
or Greece. Events, the feel they brought
remain absorbed by place. Hitler
still rants
at that street corner,
on the rooftops here. At this end
of the playing fields boys dig
for victory, Thursday afternoons,
as the propeller planes
drone, pulsing, overhead.

Still there, the long-familiar house
with the big garden, where my friend
lived and we played, where the girl
I was in love with in my teens,
and after, often visited.
A highway (multi-lane) drives through
or over where were cottages
and greens. Some things have changed about.
It's bushier, more wooded here;
beyond, by the Ouse, at Binsey,
and elsewhere,
the poplars of Cowper, Hopkins,
as the laurels, all are cut,
the elms stand dead.
The river bank is bare.

From then, I've no one left to meet,
only the graves, which ask
just so long to be viewed,
communed with there; the scene
to brush with eyes, fill
with images of early friends
distanced, dim in half-silhouette
with light behind them, as ahead,
poised at the entrance to
a tunnel of past years,
for me unable to advance,
evolve, as they did for themselves.
That done, there's no need
for a longer stay. Tomorrow I'll
check out of the hotel, be off
by car and train to what's my now.

Back from a future that has been,
I'm in the nursery beds of dreams.
I have no foolish hope
to live that course again.
But the half-expected magic
from the memory's haloing
as lightning's flicker doesn't edge
the walls and ways. It's hard to tell
just what the core now says to me
even with its auras
of remembered feeling, and
one can't help knowing it is just

a place like others, less
renewing for new's sake, forefrontish,
or impersonal than some.

Yet there's a need to see, from more
than time to time,
if only to be reassured
there's no world for me here except
with ghosts. I can go out then, free,
to where my life is now
or further may be shaped.

Oh that it were as simple, for
we cannot break the pull of soil
or skies, weathers, the atmospheres
of origins; of where we first
knew love from those who loved us
with such given help and hope
as we have not perhaps known since.

Respond somehow
to the place's call,
its lasting power to impel us
to a future, since become
that same brash modernness
which moves us on.

We like to think
we still can keep the selves
we were and are
as gifts to leave,
the more for having said,
this year again,
 'I'm back.'

A Time Of Year

People walk
in the street.
They've left
coats, gloves
behind, wear
their shadows
short.
A bus stops
in the square.
Passengers head
for the shops.

The leaves
have broken out
as lime-green fuzz
to quiver
on the trees.

An adult cat
which should
and does
know better
springs to chase
a scudding
paper cup.

Clouds spin
above the waters,
dapple earth.
I scent
flowers, rain,
possession.
        Run,
run far out there
today
to where we've
got to go.

I sight
and steer
no charted course
that threads
it all

beyond
that I see,
veer
with the pull.

The Living-Tree

Vivid clusters droop,
bold pendants from the grey
and branchy screen
of mountain ash,
scarlet berries on
November egg-shell blue,
bitter.

They're what is left
of the flowering snowy
pledges of the spring,
out of the flutter,
flurry of the green,
the promise bred
in scented breeze
and sun.

They hang as hectic fruit,
seeming not to fit,
to have outlived something,
wait

for the shrilling hiss,
the death-dark reaping cloud
to enwrap the tree
and strip,
consume the acid
residue
before they lift,
the veils of birds,

and leave
the structure cleared

for another's dreams.

December Twenty-Fourth

Much snow has fallen again over night,
and in the street outside my house
a municipal road-clearing engine,
like some thunderous man o' war, wasp-yellow

with wheels high as cliffs, deck cab and other
jutting superstructures, powers a vast,
scooped blade that parts and sprays the snow
in brackish, storm-soared waves.

And I'm reminded of a little plough
my grandfather had made, or had had made,
to clear the smaller paths about his place,
in a land where snowfalls, though occurring,
were lighter, more decorous.

It was a deepish, wooden box, shaped
like a narrow wedge, weighted
on the inside, that could be hauled
by even a six year old, delighted me.

And before it, the snow parted,
rising and curling over in delicate scrolls,
to leave a lilac, metre-broad wake
with low-walled sides, straight or zig-zaggy,
depending on how carefully one had pulled,
scraped down in patches to the bare soil

like the unlayering in today's thoughts
of my time back to that ground,
when a child was indulged by love
in its efforts with more than play
to clear a path ahead.

The Garden Seat

When very young I'd stay
at my grandparents' house.
It viewed a breathless stretch
of falling, rising land
for miles and miles.
It was a marvel
just to sit and look.

For me, too small
for more than shortest walks,
a child's
imaginative play
not out of sight,
it was a game,
with my grandmother
on a garden bench,
to watch the figures moving
in that scene.

A distant neighbour
had a tennis court.
Young people played.
Their dartings caught the eye:
forwards and backwards
drawn to focal points,
white, pastel-coloured, like
a stage magician's
handkerchiefs, or moths
at the candle dance.

These summer evenings,
afternoons, or into
autumn, I suppose
it would be, pickers stopped
to gather berries
on a far hillside.
It was a game to count
the crawling, coloured dots.
How many? Two,

another, no, four, six,
all up and down the slope.

In those days people walked—
along the main roads,
in the fields and lanes.
Some motor cars passed by
for me to watch and count,
not many, high and square,
with luggage at the back,
on roofs, a Ford, more were
hand-made, expensive, now
collectors' gems.

It was as if,
could I have thought it then,
I looked through window panes
of childhood helplessness,
deprived, so far, of time
to grow and walk
into that world beyond
I saw, of people moving,
doing things.

Shall I be able? When?
One day. Oh—one day, soon.
The years are long to be
a figure on the move
like these, free, unrestrained
it seems,
in landscapes by oneself,
to drive far off, towards conflict,
tread down fields of time.

Long years
of just such movement
as will lead one back
to the garden seat,
and to its images
I see again today.

Bicycles

The bikes cluster, flat
on the grass or, a thicket,
stacked by a park bench.
The boys and girls squat
in a group.
Light winks
from glossy paint and chrome.
Some distance off
a woman walks a dog.
On spaced seats
the elderly doze
with morning papers, or just
their hands. The sun
and heat, the drone
of a propeller
learn-to-fly-school plane
climb the blue way.

To chatter and flung limbs
the crowd is up, breaks
into flight.
The quite young
don't do what they do
for very long.
They spin
to what the day,
their time, make possible,
under the June sky.

I'm one
of the ones on the seats.

What became of my bike?
I wanted to fly,
once.
Where's left for me to go?

Back
to write this down.

La Grande Route

The spice of roses and Gauloises,
in the hot dust of the sun,
hydrangeas, paths that led,
was the breath of what would be—
at twenty-one.

Distancing yet among the châteaux
and villages
the successive roads relay
nostalgia for that scent—
at sixty-three.

What country spread
                    between?

Blanket-Shaking

Entangled in the roofscape thicketry
this December twenty-third
a sun hangs low at four o'clock
like a crimson moon.

And back across the decades
I see another
hazy, strawberry disc
through a frosty air
that shaped the breath,

and us,
wartime recruits
just posted,
in a field behind the barracks
shaking blankets.

In regulated pairs
we whipped and snapped
the leaden army issue,
folded, sneezed,
with boyish shrugs laughed off
this, branded typical,
military bafflement.

Was the sharp air deemed
to kill the bugs and microbes?
Or, mere days to Christmas,
was it a bizarre device—
more mind-numbing than,
say, cutting holly
in the leafless woods
for decking cookhouse halls—
to shift our thoughts
from the season's leave
we would not have?

But I remember the frost-honed spirits,
needled tips of hands, feet, nose,
the young blood thrusting, to which cold
was but a pleasurable goad,
and the boredom-sullen yet the real
companionship which closed its ranks
to shoulder us along
into that so improbable tomorrow.

It was the first Christmas, too,
I had not spent at home.

May Ball

Like a surprise by clowns
at earliest church, flour–
white their faces too, but with unsleep,
apologetically
or with drawn-up hauteur
they trail, black-suited, evening gowns
a wilt of harlequin yet stark,
in the cold light, the stare
from morning worshippers
of weekday work.

From the chill dampening rite
of hailing river dawn
in punt, on grass, breakfasts in villages,
they're back to hazy day,
or bed, all that's not gone
of the long throbbing band-rocked night—
the beauty, make-up, scents and wines,
drugs, sex, the guileless fun,
in halls, big tops ballooned
on college lawns.

Something we had to take
once, or more in our own
hour. The partner was important, out
of possibles a best,
perhaps, it seemed, the One—
that in most cases time would shake
off, in its smiling shrugging course,
for others, many, none.
Screened by the reach for magic
grinned the farce.

But even while we knew
of what gauze the event
was spun, this ritual tribute to our years
and social style, there came
yet at night's high a point
when, as with lightning, flared in view
some still unmet significance,

some insight, in a slant–
beamed blinding disco flash
across the dance.

What was it? Even then
what truth we couldn't say,
before the mists of weariness exhaled.
Was this our future, glimpsed,
here in epitome,
a learning without answers, when
each nature made the dreams and loves
ennui or ecstasy?
Was life no more than such
postures and moves?

Spring Planning In The Garden

Feeling we should,
we try to plan it,
labour at our life,
doubt self
on falling short.
We've seen abandoned gardens,
with the parterres blurred,
untraceable the lines
of paths where people walked
or sat, the furrows
of the dug,
raked, seeded beds,
the aims and ordering;
and have remembered
or imagined all the hours
and years of tending
left unnoted now.
In the grass and tangle
nature has imposed
another order,
and we wonder
if the plan
is for unplanned design,
or one we
cannot follow;
whether, even,
none.

A Summer Day

The green leaves strain
in a wind that flows to clear
the spirit's lag
from smouldering heat.
And I look up and through
this ash against a sky
which streams with the race
of cloud on revealed blue.
All movement, purpose:
something happening out there
it seems, to make me sense again
the pulse to go and do
what I've not done,
cannot, and know
to be illusion's sun

like those same clouds, soft, white,
appearing round,
of substance,
as the padding of a bed
or sofa, scattered
for an unknown reason, spread
on the carpet ground—
but vapour without shape,
intangible and grey;
nor do they speed.

I hear birds sing,
the thrilling larks and such,
with sounds that cause a pang,
nostalgia for the May
slipped by uncaught this year.
Some of the songs of spring
in summer are yet here
to haunt as they recall
far times of dawning trust
that everything
was possible
before the autumn hush.

We first accept what seems,
and after, when we've met
the eyes of shifting truths,
scan for a point that gives
a finished view of all.
Yet here, this day, I sight
a stirring July show
that may be nothing real
but stages passing joy.

Of Semblances

After all,
we've moved between
the ones we've known,
even well, experiences
had, throughout a life,
and caught only
the surface texture
light throws off
and never seen
the presumed eye
of things—as if among
reflections in a stream.

Strong shadows flat on snow
are virtually the tree
complete, and upside down
Claude Monet's mirrored
climbing sweep
of poplars on the Epte
are real leaves, water,
sky and cloud
in glassy shimmer
on the merging blue
green yellow
hinted peach-pink white,
to know and touch,
only a little dim
or hazier.

Turn the painting round, or
look up
to the tree.
Such known
supposed originals
are sharper,
have dimension for
more senses here, but
what do they
reflect?

Flight Of The Foiled Geese

We follow, ages of our kind,
a stream that moves in the space-time
by which we have to live while here,
like the creatures of the air,

the geese, it may be, threading skies
in the migratory days,
obedient to some inner cue,
of which no doubt they could not say,

if invited to explain,
in the least what it might mean.
Faiths, metaphysics, make it clear
(contradictory though they are).

And all seem right. Gods have come by
(with proofs of authenticity)
to this our world, with truth to tell.
Of many, only each is real.

The cry in the night of wolf or fox
startles us because it breaks
the flow of line on which we move;
is out of context, though we live

in contexts, or dimensional frames
accommodating onward trains,
linear, ubiquitous,
imposed, submerged, contiguous;

and in its frame the exploding cry,
isolated seemingly,
is yet the instant's sole effect
of nameless causes backwards linked.

Is it that we and whatever else
make neither harmony nor sense;
or a design that nothing solves
things here, that we torment ourselves

(even as intended to torment)
with sensing dissonance we can't
resolve, still less forget, with god
and creed to image us we've made,

as in the skeins of our affairs
we stream through skies of earthly years,
obey the prompts to steer our flight
ahead until our path runs out.

The Vanished

Today's motorway cuts
ahead, raw and straight.
Nothing left now,
as I flash past,
of the loop
round where that house was,
stone too,
but summer-long grass,
windspread mallow, gorse.
I knew someone
my grandfather's age
who was born there.

Demolishing the casino,
rampant machines
with prehensile clawed arms
grindingly mount rubble.
Their intense
directed pressures
further bore walls into
controlled collapse,
with smoky incense of dust
sanctifying change.
They grab and tidy, pile
thick worms of rusted wire
bedded in concrete crumble.

At the house being torn down,
rooms, indecently it seems,
are bared to view.
Layers of wallpaper show
under hued layers
of how many decades,
generations even;
patterns merged
with passion, looked at
with love, indifference,
dislike, got used to,
chosen once
with care.

The containing shells go.
What they contained
went, often, sooner.
They could not hold
a childhood, years' broods
of pleasure-moths
fluttering brief happiness,
successions of lived
domestic lives,
for ever.

Change validates
the ceased or the unaltered
we have known.
We can imagine more,
that was and may have been.
Memory safeguards longest.
But it lives only
with each one of us,
at most the race.
Where then the vanished?
We are made to crave
the permanent,
or its mirage,
to devise faiths,
philosophies which give
what the space-time can't.
Part of its flow, we move
with it, cut
across it
too.

The Necklace

It isn't easy,
looking upon land,
above all places ours,
gloried by a childhood there
or other gilding circumstance,
to know that, again far off,
we can't, more than
in photograph or memory,
embrace, possess it,
but must let the stewardship
of further and eternal time
conserve, alter, undo,
and not for us.

It isn't easy
when someone we knew well,
once, comes out of the past
with kindest, even, questions
(what have you done and what
has it been like?),
to sum, in answer, all
that made us this.
So much which counted,
then to then,
we must omit;
so much we've lost; can't tell
if it's saved, or how.

Nor easy
to accept the way time puts
a life together,
makes you view a whole,
falsely, it seems, abstracting,
threading beads of us
on the long-stretched cord,
to fasten, make at last
the round complete.

Moving Into A Landscape

I look at this country.
Close up there is a tree,
gnarled by the years.
A road or lane runs past it,
narrowing in miles
towards the blue
of distance. The tree,
we've been taught to fancy,
enwraps secrets, clutches time.
The road, seeming to beckon,
is an emblem of the dreamed
advance to otherness.

If I were in mystical vein
I'd see some believed truth
lying beneath this upper layer
the senses speak of.
I don't of course mean just
a geological sub-structure
almost surfacing,
half-cubistically
as in Cézanne,
but a system of some inner
being, goings on,
of which these objects of our sight
are hints and signs.

The young know they don't know,
but believe for a while
there's truth to be known.
So much they may learn,
for there are some certainties.
But they are not satisfied.
It must be something more,
they say, tell us what it is.

Having travelled the road
only to find
the blue distance recedes
(but even now is always there,
ahead),
clutching our own time's secrets,
we've gained as yet
no panoramic viewing-place.
What if, we have to ask,
there are repeated
physical sub-strata
like the ones we sense,
and then, below, beyond those, more,
but nothing else.

Conditioned as we are,
have we a need to make believe
a core reality exists
that we may glimpse.
Or, being true
does it, at breaks, thin places
in our casing shell,
by showing through
proclaim itself?

The Faces Of Spain: 1986

Elderly, old,
they're featured this year
by magazines and TV,
with the faces of age,
brown-mottled, sagged, or drawn
by that or some later field,
just life, but mainly time,
in the probing colour of now,
the roses, the sun
of today's Spain.
Beside them are shown
themselves of five decades past,
sometimes in startling beauty, gone,
at least the radiance of their young,
firm, trackless skin, the eyes lit
from the inner dream.

The picture appeared
a chiaroscuro then,
right against wrong,
as the dark shades,
the searing light
of the contended hillsides,
coverless plains
in the black and white
film footage shown
of those events and days.

On soil long nurturing the strain,
a people seeded, harvested
a newer kind of holy war.
It bared the ordinary folk
and their beliefs and kin, their homes
and bodies to the bullet's whine
in town and village battled through,
as the bomb rains screamed.
That was not, even if foreseen
from the alignments ranged,
too abhorrent to deter
the cause from scattering
this method's customary shards

of broken things and lives.
It may be that the given chance
then to rehearse the century
could not be passed.

It was the manhood trial for some,
late for that earlier time. It lured
the ones who live by tenets,
like a star. To partisans
from other lands it was
a different waging, not
of nations but beliefs,
set out upon the board
of this one state, drawing
the self-created soldiery
whose countries did not want them,
then, for home, or to be here.
Creators, thinkers went,
and in their words or art
lastingly gave issues form.
For others, unconcerned,
or not yet old enough
to be a part, it threw
and merged its shadow
with the other deeper glooms
then chequering the day
of 'thirties boyhood,
brushed with heavy wings
the sunlit plains of innocence.

They think of their dead comrades,
wonder at being still here.
As not all can,
they had at least lived once
primed with the heady charge
of sacrifice, idealism's fire.
Perhaps the life spent since
has shown them what it may
or yet may not have been,
has shaped to winter clarity
what was hazed by summer sun
and battle smoke,
or haloed then.

'How did you truly feel?
What do you think today?'
Their words in answer speak
a resignation,
bitterness, some passion left.
The old eyes of each one
veil with something sad
for what is over, unresolved;
friends' lives, or victory
later missed again, or kept;
but most that ardent zeal
fused with their flame of youth
and brave-new-worldish time.

'What was the war in Spain?'

Today's young ask. Madrid,
Toledo's Alcazar,
Bilbao, Guernica.
How to explain,
feeling as we do
regret, anger, despair
at the eruptive, epidemic frays,
so far contained but
dangerous
besetting us at will,
that like diseases gnaw
at the whole flesh
of our choice to live.
Were the efforts vain;
does this age see
only the sacrificial gestures
heroism made.
Were only the beliefs,
the courage real.

We watch it
as a piece of history,
know it was clouded out
by what would come.
Its close was a beginning.
It was a forward symptom
of the greater agony
and writhings towards an end.

It will not repeat itself,
even in fancied analogues.
It saddens, as all fate
which after-wisdom can avert.
We trace in it
the choreography
of the grouped and shifting
ideologies
and power bloc choruses
rehearsing for the next
full-scale and imminent
production, since long-running,
of this century's dance of death.

But if that's all, why then
the living stir of pride
at seeing, hearing them.
At the horizons of their hell
the incandescent vision
of the bettered life
stood in the skies.
They once possessed what we
take from ourselves, to leave
only an apathy
or fear too dire
to apprehend, confront.

Where is that force from love,
from fervour, from the needed hate
of self-perpetuating means,
compulsions to destroy.

As energy
may it be present yet,
moving between times,
directionless,
waiting to return
and beam itself again.

November Eleventh

Today
the ink-soaked clouds
and lurid gleams brood
in a Vlaminck sky
disturbed and desolated as
a Flanders warscape,
'Menin Road', or 'Totes Meer'
of another fray.

Again we think of then
and them, and of all wars
our nature makes
that had their way.

But had their end.
Organic matters torn
and spilled were at the worst
absorbed in history
and earth and put
imaginably
to some further use.
Always exhaustion
slowed the hand,
cried for a stop.

And,
till our time,
the ravaged, grief-drawn face
knew it could turn
from horror, fear,
and lift for balming hope
to the green again
and blowing land,
the light, the air.

Passes

i

I walk in the country
this day out,
pause at a gate.
The youth on the tractor
crawls ploughing up
the hillside field;
trails furrows and birds.
He is spring.

He's there eternally
in the landscape
of freedom
I long to inhabit.
He's winter and autumn,
summer.

I move on.

ii

Ploughing time's come round.
Soil's about right,
drying, not too dry.
Another year,
day after day.
It's like this then,
is it?—sitting,
driving, lonely hours,
each time different and
the same.
A life.

A man stands
at the gate down there
framed in the hedges.
Stranger
from cities

the world outside
I can't escape to.

.

Gone again.
He doesn't
exist now.

Tomorrow
the twelve acre.

Day To Life

The neighbours' cars
start up.
Doors slam
at ten to nine.
As usual
children pass
along the street
to school.

Round four
and five
the children,
neighbours, cars
come back again,
all looking
just the same.

Something,
more or no more
than time shows,
has happened
to them
in between.

The Solitudes

He sits up, smokes,
a figure all dark
in a suit of some kind,
hair page-boy long,
black, matted, greased,
like a travesty foul
of Olivier's Richard the Third
(with or without a limp).
Rolls suddenly over,
lies on the bed of earth
seeded, raked, and bare
between phases of yellow,
white and purple
season-long bloom
of a traffic isle
in Juan-les-Pins.
Kip down there for the night?
You still see odd ones like this
here, and elsewhere.
In the 'sixties, 'seventies,
it was the young, in groups,
sold out to American cults,
because they wanted it.
Now, in ones or twos,
it's older, darker stuff.
They have it,
want it or no.

With his ash-grey skin,
eyes sunk in pits,
grime and seeming hopelessness
did he never recover
from the 'sixties,
or is he the derelict victim
of self, events,
from some later time?
Age indeterminable.

Replete with what it takes,
wine, drugs of whatever sort,
fierce principle, ideals

lost or caught, plain hunger even.
The causes,
mechanisms of his style
are not apparent here.

From the café opposite
I end a last drink
and watch,
all white:
light slacks, shirt,
in the summer heat,
clean, I suppose
with awaiting me
my four star hotel room
and if I want it
another, bedtime, bath.

No. He's got up,
not stopping there all night,
passed with surprising alacrity
like some scuttling black spider
out of sight,
into his further darkness
that may,
who knows,
and may it,
contain some light.

And I go now
back to my own
night
of self-sustaining comforts
at the end of a day,
career, and soon perhaps
a life
adequate in the world's eyes,
respectable, if unremarked,
to solitude like,
I presume, his,
and a certain dark emptiness
I've never managed,
will never manage, to fill.

Why am I not moved to go after him,
find him, say
'What can I do that will help,
if indeed there's anything?'

Where, I can only wonder,
did we each,
if we did,
go wrong.

Cottage Smoke

Above the trees, from her cottage
hugged in the glade,
her smoke signed to the neighbourhood.
Someone was there.

For her, unmarried, by herself,
it had been home.
The heir, a nephew, did not come
to live in it.

Sun rayed cold boughs, sequined June leaves.
Birds risked the long-
closed threshold, printing snow. Dust clung
to window panes,

rimed the still furnishings. At spaced
breaks of the year
scouts with leave to camp would enter,
raise the smoke wreath.

And those left who knew might fancy,
was her deep quiet
broken once in a while by that
laughter of youth?

jog
ger

time's im
prov ing
can in
crease my
dis tance
same cars
ev 'ry
day to
work   last
min ute
most could
run   walk
an y
way   kids
too   a
shame   their
bod ies
will break
down in
mid dle
life if
not be
fore
          they
see me'n'
smile as
they drive
past all
warm an'
dry

That fitness nut
They say it hurts
the tendons, joints,
heart, head, and feet

this rain
an' chil
ly wind

why don't
i give
it up

to mor
row i
can sure
bet ter
my time

Friendly News

...Sylvanus got promotion, and they said
that he's by far the youngest and the best
executive they've ever ever had
in all their firms. Tamara married just
last week. Her Caspar's in the City—stocks—
with up his sleeve an even bigger card
(I mustn't breathe a *word* but—*politics!!*).
And Jocelyn's Hera now expects their third,
to join a girl and boy, Katina, Tratty
(Tristan), six and three, fair, blue-eyed, tall,
the brightest and, so very, *very* pretty.
But—we look for greatest things from Ju
(lia). *Head Girl* of School. Hope after all
this time that life goes fairly well with you?

The Models

To the caress of costly scent,
low music, the presenter's voice,
they pose revealed—
the models at staged fashion shows.
In phalanxes or groups
or ones or twos
relentlessly they march
along the ramp
as if they'd trample you
to high heel death,
then check and turn.
Like savage sexy cover girls
with glare of baleful eyes,
pout of their pumped-up lips,
they menace you to buy.
In flaring draperies,
dark, relentless as the Furies,
wielding their unseen whips
they swirl, sadistic,
stride, twitch hips,
tower up, feet wide apart, to wither
with disdainful sneer,
shrug and recede
in their never-before (or since?)
seen dress-house fantasies.

On cue
they then withdraw
docile as deer.

They're like the notions
for our writing, or our lives,
as these advance and crowd.

As ever, there is little
we could wear—

but now and then
material,
a line, a cut
that we can see
adapted to our shape.

A Day In Amber

Hard to know what touches off
memory. With this blue,
cold winter sky
blends another, up beyond
the whispering restiveness
of summer-laden trees.
They met, and arched the stream
as bottle-green it glided, slapped
below our punt-load mix
of men and women.

We moored at a strategic point
on the Cherwell's banks, and walked
across the Parks, our feet stirring
the rising, dry, warm hay-smell
from cut grass, to someone's digs
for tea. Later, back to the punt
again—there safely waiting.
In this progress between water
and meadows, we were like
the amphibious river-bank
creatures foraging (that summer
we lived much on the water).
Then upstream into the evening—
pub suppers of cider, beer,
whatnot, and the return, at length,
in the damp air, and acrid balm
exhaled from the river and night,
a moontrack silver on the black
and glistening path.

It was the late 'forties,
an age—as times well past
are dubbed—of innocence.
This too will be,
one day.

We were at the phase
when the young go in groups
to inspirit self-assurance,

when we lived a collective life.
Love came into it: the
expected amorous
expectations. There were sundry
pairings off, for immediate
future satisfactions,
though I forget who was with whom.
Does it matter (if at the time,
violently) now?

For us, free yet, just, it was still
all ahead, like the sun specks
sprinkling through leaves on water,
the ambitions, chosen pursuits,
the careers, vocations,
marriages or liaisons
that would hold or fail.
And, oddly, now that I've been
most of the way out, tremors
of that live expectancy stir
as part of the remembering.
Those same people disappeared
into their lives and the years,
to submit to the usual process
of changing and being the same.
I've kept up, lastingly, with none.
I might not know them in the streets.
So what did it mean,
this being brought together
in what retrospection says
were magical moments:
some illusionist's trick show
of significant conjunction,
some deceiving look of permanence,
a charade that knew it was one
even as it played? I don't think
we said as we crossed the Parks
'we are living a magical moment',
but we stuck, made an event, together,
so there would have been something.

And the occasion
had its import. It has stayed,
a fixity set
in the gold of then.

We were experiencing—what:
each other, youth, companionship,
the summer beauty, love, and hope?
I don't know everything it meant,
beyond merely
the recalled day, and
the entreating memory.

The experience was
the recollection now.

Where Are They Now?

Old boy, alumnus groups, fund raisers,
when it may be necessary
or desirable to know
will circulate the question, dropped

in the letter-box on a spring day
as we're about to cut the grass,
go fishing in the local stream.
We also have this thought sometimes

about those two or more who have
slipped through the net of ken or records
to unplanned oblivion
or chosen limbo, have achieved,

by wish or by default, annulment
of a past we shared. Not dead,
it's likely. Death has its own voices,
and proclaims itself at once,

or else eventually. But vanished
into other lives, long lived,
in far off regions, isolated
river pools. It is as with

some closer friends. When did we cease
to meet, to write? There was no quarrel,
or caused breach. For some years letters
passed, with lessening frequency

as more and more the persons and
events discussed, thoughts, aims expressed,
seemed to become concerns of
mere strangers. Christmas cards, then one

or other stopped. Addresses changed,
were lost. While we like railway lines
keep parallel a time in the same
place, as long our closeness runs.

The threads of our tracks, surprisingly
it seems, have not crossed since.
I really must get back in touch.
But how begin? And usually

not now. I will when I've more time,
or when I next meet Babington,
who'll know. Is it that we hesitate
to start again: embarrassment,

or doubt that there'll be anything
in common left between two, now,
so different selves, and life-formed beings?
Better leave... in case we find

nothing is there of that once other
whom we knew. In moving on
we've walked with later friends along
the river bank, according to

our feelings, needs, just as we did
in youth, although back then we thought
that friendships lasted, did not hang
on time or place or circumstance.

Where are they now? They're in the lives
they've made, or have had made for them,
somewhere out there, and wondering,
perhaps, as I do, where am I?

The Clocks Go Back

It's a morning lit by the stillness of gold.
My garden trees are globes of powdered gold.
The sun sprays beams of golden dust through leaves,
gives the feel of the summer that ends here.
The empty globe of the day contains us,
sounds silently like a washed prayer,
waits to be filled.

I cannot fill it, though I stretch
and breathe in deeply to absorb it.
Does activity fill it: the doings
we see about us of all humans?
The globe of gold rotates, unfissured, with the day
then switches off.

The clocks go back tonight.

The rhythmic taps, startling for a moment,
make me go to the window. It's the branch
on the pane. After the blood
of sunset a wind has got up. A tree,
all gold with some green still, in agitation
shakes out a street-lamp's caged moonlight
into the dusk. Brown leaves scatter in whorls
along the ground. Dry rustle is the smell
of the night. Three youths go by, hands thrust
in pockets, shoulders hunched against the cold,
lean on the wind, hurry to pleasures, dreams.

The streets are scoured and bare, white, cleansed,
with a sense of new beginnings as in spring.
It is a kind of spring, year's death that starts
a life beyond the returning world
of winter lights.

The clocks go back.

Our lives go back a step of the travelled way
to our beginnings, in this cyclical nudge
towards our other start.

Entr'acte: Part Of An Untold Old Tale

See

how tall the sun is   sleep a little here
in the beach umbrella's shade   while mummy writes
the sea's all silver-grey   with heat

...we're here
it's bright and crackling   no crowds yet
with Easter past   He sent us down   generous
I have to say   He's to the mountains   I expect
with her...

                    No darling not into the sun
again   you've made it angry   likes the place
to itself at noon   later we'll play
on the shore

....so now we wait   funny   just four
years   our wedding day   as you remember
Silvie dear   he's too little to remember
much I hope of all the...

How to write and tell them   how begin again
soon a divorced woman   neither young nor special
with a child

                    I have a child   I've that

meanwhile

the sun's warm   sleep and forget
what you've not
known
               and wait
                    and grow

Heat levitates white buildings   coloured
national flags   electric as frost   a frost
at noon

A youth and girl embracing walk the sand

Their arms laced behind them make a cross

Still farther off

a boy plays by himself   at the sea's edge

A Tourist's Passing Thoughts

In this church at Beaugency
(small, romanesque)
the marriage was dissolved
(a plaque proclaims)
of Eleanor of Aquitaine
to her husband king of France
(and which was he?—
a summer tourist's bag is light
in facts that can't be checked
upon the spot, as well as gear).

Today's bridge did not span the Loire.
Perhaps this same broad river passed
in a different course,
but it was there.

If present, then,
might she (he, they—
would one, or both,
neither attend?)
have listened to the river's voice
distinctive above rivers everywhere,
this sunny, ceaseless pressing hiss
of shallow flowing over sand,
so that she'd know
one day at Chinon
the waters of Vienne ran deeper
with a darker, hollow sound?

Or were they thinking only
of their farther destinies
for which that day
would set them free.

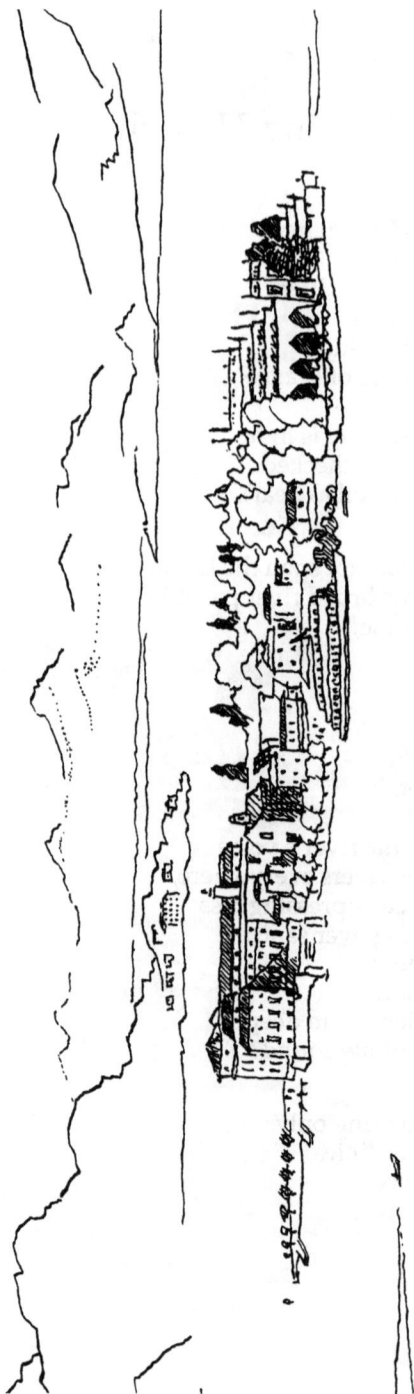

Isola Bella, Lake Maggiore

Isola Bella

I come here late in life, at last approach
this lure not missed by all Grand Tourist eyes
of then and now, having seen at the right time
(I mean in youth) Léman, Vierwaldstättersee,
Varese, Como, Nemi, Garda. Now
Maggiore, dazzling blue and gold, white, green
in the Italian May. From Stresa's pier
our ferry-load descends upon the isle,
where crowds already mill. The gardens first,
I think, to get the lay-out of the place.

Time past for me to be caught, stilled in snapshot,
as a lover with the lovers here,
against the grotto-shell, shell-grotto backdrop
of the Theatre, with pure white peacocks,
or, the blue of lake behind them, leaning
on the Belvedere Avenue's
stone balustrade, or dwarfed by mountain banks
of blossoming azaleas,
magenta, yellow, white and pink, and this
in no way bothers me. Rather I sigh
with a relief (now seeing in my mind
the yet, somewhere or other, extant pictures
of a bygone love, where we resplendently
stand draped with the cascading fountain veils
of Villa d'Este) for the peace
from such emotions' clamour to rejoice,
and wonder at the fantasy of this
fantastic and fantastically lovely
place, a vision wrought of magic, if
no baseless fabric, insubstantial pageant,
spelling magic still.

> ...who were they, then,
> these Borromeos?...
>
> Nobles, princes, one
> a saint, and virtual kings

Isola Bella : Upper Terrace

of all this lakeland.
They...

...think you can manage dear
these flights up to the eighth
ninth and top terraces?
They say that there are ten.
The view...

We climb up
this inverted bedstead this construction
of child's blocks this stepped and flat-topped
pyramid this Mayan temple, poop
of the ship this isle was made to look like.
Hanging gardens, tiered in granite, rivalling those,
it's said, of Egypt, China, Babylon.
Lords of this lakeland, world in itself
where life lives on its waters and along
its edges, inland, in a hundred towns
and villages all up and down the map
for more than fifty miles.

   ...*Magnolia Grandiflora*...

...My, the view. What's over there?

The Isola Madre
and I think Pallanza...

...How the sun beats and beats.
There is no shade up here...

...they call it 'Garden of Love'
look down
and see its matched geometry...

I like the central lily pond...

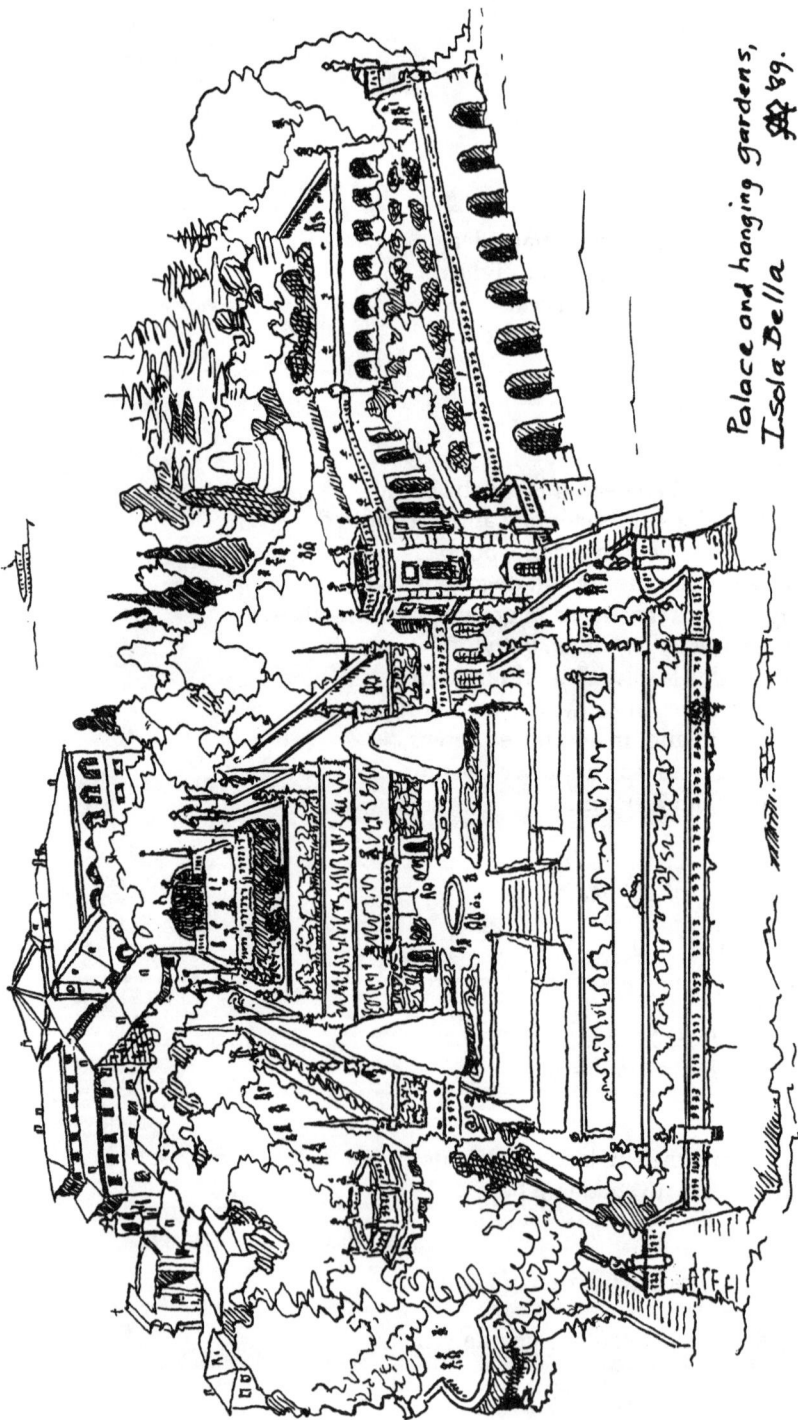

Palace and hanging gardens,
Isola Bella

Remarks the great (especially writing men)
have made about it are preserved, well known.
Barrès and Bertolotti, Charles de Brosse,
the bishop Burnet, Dickens, and Dumas,
Flaubert, Manzoni (or was that of Como?),
English J. A. Symonds, and Stendhal.
With *Tristan* just created, Wagner writes
that here he found a peace, Turner and Corot
painted it.

    ...Mom can we go now?
    This place is *weird*.

    We're here. We can't get off
    before the next boat comes.
    Besides, it's famous. We
    just *have* to see it...

    What're all them statues and
    the things all stickin' up?
    It's like a Disneyland without...

    Well, that's a unicorn—
    and ornamental
    slender obelisks...

    I'm *tired*...

    Tomorrow we'll drive on
    to reach Milan. You'll see there...

    ...*Camphora Officinalis*...

    ...why did we have to come?...

    ...the *Mexican Agave*.
    Fruits just once...

Why come to be pressed among crowds like these?
Flocks of children brought to view such shrines perched
on the boat at Stresa, shrilled like starlings

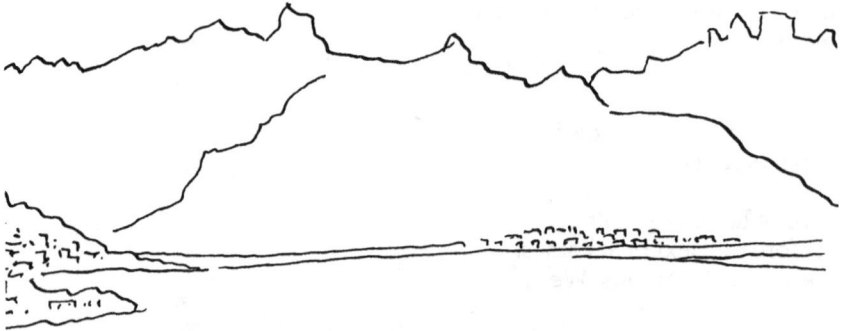

Borromeo Palace and gardens,
Isola Bella. Beyond,
Isola dei Pescatori

all around and over everybody,
caring little what they saw in this
sweet break from lessons. In the end (the sail
is very short) you had to laugh.
The isle is full of noises, sounds
in many tongues, a few of which one knows.
It's the appeal of past authority
and wealth, their sting, their power to patronize,
oppress, removed by time. The beauty left,
which only power and wealth could make
when this was made. Here is the fashioning
of nature, art, of nature into art,
to mould a shelter of serenity,
a wonder also, flaunting taste and skill
at their command, to silence betters, equals
into envy, awe the rest.
One sees it in that century and the next
at Vaux-le-Vicomte and Versailles, the Schönbrunn,
Schwarzenberg, Juvara's Stupinigi,
Neumann's Würzburg Residenz, Benrath,
the Nymphenburg of Munich, Sans Souci,
Schloss Weissenstein (or Pommersfelden), Brühl,
at English Hampton, Chatsworth, Castle Howard.
They built to wear around them beauty, space,
far in excess of need.
What need...? O, reason not the need.

     ...Of course I said to her,
     dear Jane, you really must
     confront him with her—that
     you know of their affair...

     ...but Michel, no, it is
     quite cramped, confined...
     At Fontainebleau, at Vaux,
     Versailles, we have the space,
     the vistas...

     ...Island Beautiful
     but 'Isola Isabella'

it was once, named for
the wife of Carlo III...

The water is like satin and shot silk,
with undercurrents making sheeny shimmer
in the sun. Green, white, and brown, the islands
lie and float on prussian blue, which shades
to peacock, azure, nearer shore.
It's almost noon. Hot stillness hangs above.
Small craft and ferries, moving, draw their wakes
like arrow-heads across the water's smooth
yet wrinkled, slowly-crawling face. Heat wafts
up from the gravel, crunched
by casual, curious feet.

...it's the baroque. We've learned
all that in fine-art school.
Of nature, buildings, merged
in one great unity
to make a spectacle,
and foregrounds, backgrounds, axes,
symmetries, inside
extending outside, parterres,
fountains, statues, water,
terraces and vistas,
balanced masses, movement
and dramatic thrusts.
A stage for human acts,
admitting fantasy.
This is a fantasy
suggested by the shape
the island had. A challenge
to impose the features
of a great demesne
on this restricted space.
The fiction of a ship.
House at the prow and
pleasure at the helm, as
gardens... *Excuse me!*...

Oh Christalynn, you know
just such a lot.

I've studied it, Jo Ann.
It interests me. I'd like
to write about it, draw.
Maybe a book...

You'll paint it up?

I've made quick sketches.
Anything of this
must fight for life
just so as to escape
banality.

You'll make them all your own—
original, I'm sure.

I hope. I just can't wait
to get to Rome.
Here it's domestic, there
ecclesiastical
baroque. Some lunch before
we catch the boat at two?

The island-ship at anchor rides the lake
for ever through the changing light and cycles
of the years. Its passengers arrive,
and they depart not quite the same, impressed
with images of a created thing
they've loved, not understood, disliked, but which
has left them not forgetful, unaware.
The lower mountains, plunging, ring the lake,
some snow-tipped still. From Monte Mottarone
far above, the view extends, westwards
and north, with the conditions right,
to outer giants ranged beyond, the Strahlhorn,
Monte Rosa, Täschhorn, Fletschhorn, Dom,
Leone, and, in the farther Bernese Alps,
the Jungfrau. Irresistible the spell
of lakes. For something seems to come to rest,
as into them, like rivers, flow our stress
and tensions, strife, to surface level calm
as pleasing dreams which rise with glints of light
off waters. Little islands in the lakes

are like ourselves in isolation, worlds
reduced we may control, at least can see
as wholes. And above all, the high mountains,
if we have need, or will, or power to soar.

......think, Mark, Napoleon
and Josephine were here
in seventeen ninety-seven.
That room, the very bed...
It's so romantic. Then
she came again—alone.
How sad...

Claire dear, I *was* thinking,
couldn't we—
I mean go off alone
somewhere along the lake,
Locarno, Belgirate,
Lesa, for a night
or two? Could tell the parents
it's a party of us—
friends we've met...

They have been through the house. I'm round again
via the Grand Avenue, the giant
greenhouse, to the exit I came in by
somehow not being stopped. I got it wrong.
You are supposed to do the palace first.
I rather start by looking at a place
in its environs. This great garden sings
with names botanical: *Camellia
Reticulata, Pinus Montezumae,
Aurum Maculatum, Quercus Suber,
Liquidamber Styracifluum
Cupressus Arizonica*. I now
go down and through, on this west side,
the streets of houses, restaurants, hotels,
shops, landing-quays, a village which retains
a toe-hold on this isle so richly filled,
to reach the palace, roughly cruciform,
Roman, basilican, square, massive, high,
with rust-tiled roofs, walls grey and pearly. Glimpsed

Medals Room, Borromeo Palace

through stately windows open to the sun,
framed panel screens of turquoise brushed with gold,
the water laps below the terraces
and balconies. A palace built on coolness
and on blue, for summer pleasures, peace,
refreshment of the spirit, hopeful ease.

....This fine apartment is
the Medals Room, called so
from those ten spaced and gold
medallions, bas-relief,
along the cornice, by
Zanelli. Happenings in
San Carlo Borromeo's
life. The paintings are
of Seicento. See
Vitaliano VI
by Milanese. Chairs
in Gobelin. The stucco
and wood carvings, white
and gilt, of ceilings, walls
are quite especially rich.
Do not omit to observe,
before departing out,
the central chandelier
of fine Murano glass...

This chamber, this high vault,
in which we stand is called
the Great, or Banquet, Hall,
a formal meeting-place
for the occasions of
solemnity. It is
a room with central plan,
four-lobed, proportioned up.
You please now to observe
the four piers' thrust to roof,
surmounted by four lateral
semi-vaults, and by
the central, highest one,
the dome...

It soars up three full floors to the whole height
of this north-west (or transept) wing, in part
projecting, apse-like, from its front.
Sublime effect of captured, echoing space
and air, all bird's-egg blue of walls, and white
of stucco: fine rococo tendrils, clusters,
swags, heraldic lambrequins, cartouches,
the gilt of bosses. It's like being inside
an emptied, towering wedding-cake...

                    ...Observe
          high up, four symbols of
          the Borromeos, wrought
          in gilded wood
          with angels as supporters,
          lemon, camel, bit,
          and unicorn. Upon
          the dome, the motto of
          the house, the single word
          'Humilitas'...

First re-adjust the necks, and pass along
the enfilade of state apartments, eyes,
already saturate with charge of sights,
in weakened self-defence now glancing off
importunate, demanding gleams of textures:
stuffs—brocades, silks, velvets, tapestry,
the golds and marbles, floor mosaics, soft glass,
fine woods and leathers, crystals, porcelains;
of shapes—the cabinets and bronzes, clocks,
and secrétaires, busts, consoles, candelabra,
mirrors, vases, pedestals, and urns,
the paintings by known masters, secular
and holy subjects, portraits, landscapes, shrined
in deeply-wrought, light-torturing golden frames.

Ridiculous perhaps to see at once,
in minutes, hours at most, what was intended
not for such processional exposure
but the gracing, comfort, elevating, joy
of single, private times in special sectors
of the whole. The swift and ranging conquest
of the land, this capture, senses' rape
of objects, this gross swallowing, this gorging,
gluttony, demands a price—aesthetic
surfeit and museum nausea,
fatigue. But rather than not see, some choose,
are glad, to pay.

        ...is called
the Music Room because
of instruments at that
far wall, a clavichord
and spinet, under glass
a viol da gamba, double
lute. Are pictures by
Pieter ('Tempest') Muller.
In this room it was
in April 1935
the Stresa Conference held,
when Mussolini, Mac
Donald, Laval agreed
to keep the *status quo*
between the powers. You see
a copy of result
upon that wall. We go
now to Napoleon Room...

     ...I've heard of Mussolini. Who
were the other ones?...

Spring, nineteen thirty-five. Dim memories
and echoes from my boyhood days.
Perhaps a headline in a newspaper

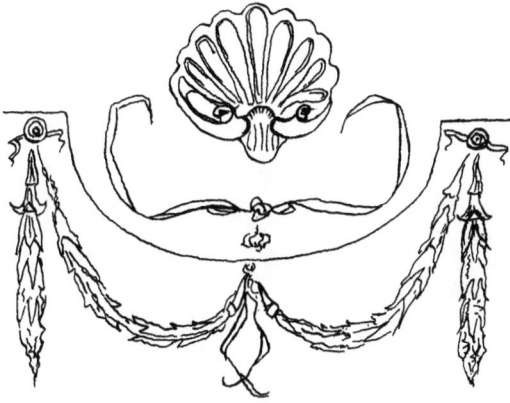

recalled, although I'm not quite sure. Some words
on wireless news. What was I doing, feeling
then? though I remember where.
An earlier 'peace in our time'. It was
that same year Mussolini sprang
his Abyssinian war. To most of these
here now, it is not even history.
And is it just as well that such things pass,
and fade from human ready memory.
We are reluctant to keep fast
realities of suffering, pain, and wars,
although perhaps we should, lest we forget.
Here we rejoice in that which has survived
so much of change, turmoils. Something in us
will see it does, for it is needed by us
as the blood of life.

> ...and after Campo Formio,
> which treaty gave control
> to him of Italy,
> Napoleon with his then
> wife, Josephine, slept here...

And did, it may be. Though like England's queen,
Elizabeth the First, Napoleon seems
to have slept too often everywhere.

      ...again in 1805
      as Emperor and Empress.
      She, when put aside,
      returned in 1812,
      alone. In this alcove
      you see the bed...

All conquerors, dictators, for a time
at least, acquire the use of palaces
like this (the best of course must be theirs first),
sometimes even appreciating them.
Napoleon, it's said, loved Fontainebleau...

      ...Amalia, my guidebook
      gives an architect
      Crivelli for the house
      who planned or started it,
      but others also mentioned
      are—Pietro Barca,
      and Richini of
      Milan, Castelli and
      Carlo Fontana, gardens
      laid by Barca and
      Vismara. But they seem
      to be unsure. It is
      not satisfactory...

      Eleonora, it
      may be that many were
      engaged, so now it is
      not clear precisely who
      did what, and when...

      ...it says all this
      was making from
      twenty to seventy-one

of sixteen hundreds, when
a great inauguration was...

...just ten years after that
of our own Vaux-le-Vicomte's...

...here the paintings by
Francesco Zuccarelli
(1702-'88)
of Borromeo lands
and castles. This the rock
fortress of Angera,
Arona...

...What a lovely room...

Yes Penny. Zuccarelli
spent some time in England,
twice. They liked his work.
His skyscapes, feathery trees
had an effect on later
landscape schools, they say
on Constable...

Indeed a lovely room. Quite small.
Only the Zuccarellis, green, white, blue,
in slender, smooth and curving golden frames,
the figured velvet-covered, gilded chairs,
the pebble-mosaic floor, a chandelier.
Its windows give towards the south, on long
grass terraces, protected by, to west,
the 'nave' wing of the palace, eastwards, open
to the lake, with parterres, delicate,
restrained, scroll-work in flowers, white pebbles
on the grass, a tracing too of that
one family motto word again,
improbably 'Humilitas'.

We look about, make of it what we can,
relate the unfamiliar to the known
at home, seize on some fact, or thought,
comparison, with that within our own
experience, fall back on national, local
referents to make what is bewildering
meaningful. And so we learn,
even still, within a Europe blended
in one greater whole. And so it seems
a regionalism must remain a force
affecting all our lives. It's where we are
and have our being that for most remains
the core reality, although this shortness
of our bounded vision must reduce
all else to limits of our little range,
even in the sweep of broad and challenging
assertions such as this.

...fancy, the walls are shells.
How different and how cute.
Oh Sherman, make sure now
you get some real good pictures
of all this to show
back home...

So, to remaining visitable parts
and out again. The curious, shell-encrusted
grotto-rooms beneath, adorned by
folk-craftsmen, just above the water, refuge
into coolness from the summer heats—
like inner chambers of some coral reef
submerged, all grey and white, with water's shadows
moving faintly on the ceilings, walls—
and things on show, a model of this island,
family forts, some ancient pottery
and weapons, iron tools.
Then last, upstairs again, the gallery
which leads you out, hung with the tapestries
in silk and gold of fighting beasts, both wild
and mythological, in sylvan scenes.

The light of, now, late afternoon
slants over waters, pulls the shadows out
from garden objects, distant hills,
and floods a wash of violet over all.

I head towards the exit, twice passed through
today, and out and down to find the boat
for Stresa.

> ...Careful Grandmother,
> this path is steep. I hope
> you're not too tired...
>
> Tired, yes. But what of that.
> I've seen this place again.
> I've always thought of it,
> the terraces, the gardens,
> and the flowers, the house
> of course, the lake.
> We came here, Charles and I,
> while on our wedding journey,
> sixty years this year.
> I wanted to return,
> but lately did not feel
> I ever could. So grateful,
> Geoffrey, Susan, dears,
> for taking me. So kind

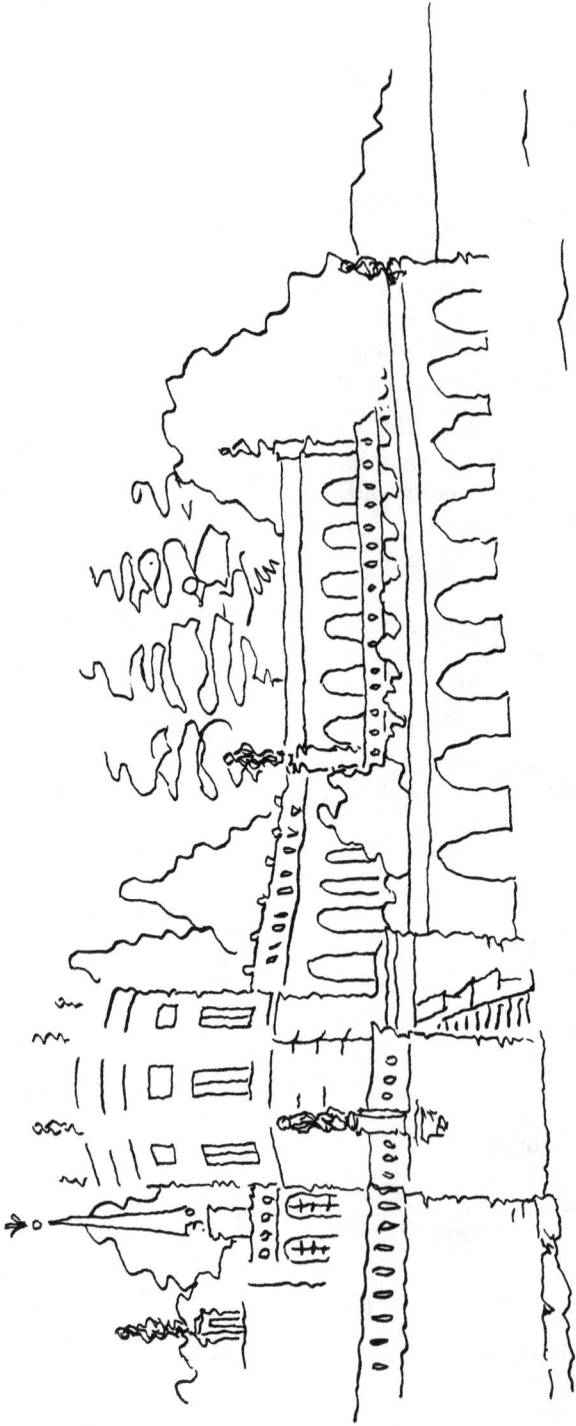

Isola Bella:
Belvedere Tower

and patient, giving days
you might have passed with friends.

No friend we'd rather
pass them with...

I think of lovely places
seen, and those not known
I'll never visit now.
But this today has been
your gift to me, a gift
of time that has been saved
from time.
So sorry not to have managed
all the steps...

I've spent much of a lifetime visiting
abroad places of beauty, interest
of one kind or another, somewhere almost
every year, if not for long. What impulse?
Gratifying an historic sense,
aesthetic taste, which like to cull, first-hand,
constructive triumphs of the past which still
remain existing and accessible.
There's that. But it's also a compensating
for a something missed in life, fulfilment
of a different kind, some permanent
relationship, perhaps, not found; a chase
of as yet undiscovered satisfactions
which the latest object to unveil
may cede, new town, new region, building,
to unclothe with trembling eyes, while they,
indifferent courtesans, unmoved, unmoving,
bored, stand of necessity resigned.
Collector's impulse too. A saving up
of senses' palpable experience
of what's remarkable or beautiful
as store for winter of commitment to
more barren places, forfeit or sold hours.
Often one had the sense on parting from
a new rewarding find of having missed
some glory, from fatigue or else decision

not to spoil the feast with surfeiting.
'I'll make a point of seeing that next time.'
But we have seldom visited again
even the most favourite of the wonders.
There are always more.
For those who pace the world, as some have wish
and opportunity to do, the truth
one day stabs in that now our years run fast.
Either we let new magnets draw, or yield
to weakening force of those that still await
avowed returns, not both.
Some places we shall never see,
some never see again.

                        ...I wish
            we could have taken slips
            of all the plants. So many
            rare, exotic shrubs
            and trees...

            And be arrested or
            thrown out. They wouldn't
            likely grow at home.
            Besides, the customs...

            ...angel, I'm quite hungry.
            Where shall we dine tonight?
            At the hotel or drive
            along the lake to...

            ...trailing after guides
            exhausts one so. You're swept
            along—no chance to pause
            and look...

            At Castle Howard you don't.
            They've guides in every room,
            who talk about what's there.
            You take your time.

            How civilized...

...Tomorrow it's Locarno,
right to the lake head
almost. See, on the map...
Takes most part of a day
up there and back by boat.

That's into Switzerland.
We'll need our passports then?

Dunno. I'll ask the ticket
clerk when we get back...

...But Christopher why now?
Why tell me now. Oh God
it isn't fair after .
all this today this lovely
day in this... It can't
be true. Tell me it isn't
true... We can't be finished,
over...

Wasn't sure myself
till now. I thought it fairer
that you know. I'm sorry if...

Oh God. I can't go home
from here alone...

No need. Don't cry. Oh please...

...At night in our hotel
the lounge is full my dears,
I mean but *full*, of Germans,
coach-loads, not a seat
left to be had for us.
They must do everything
together, so *collective*.
Then of course they *sing*.
They do it awfully well.
They've voices, harmony,
all that, but then I mean
who *wants* it?...

...grinding down the poor.
How many people died
I wonder, building all
of this...

Oh Raymond, there you are
again. And how d'you know
that any died...

There's bound to have been some.
Those days...

Look Raymond, here's our boat...

They're all around me. People. I'm among them
on a day like this. I'm with them, yet
not of them. I'm now spared the tensions, crises
close relationships will weave as nets.
Unlike that lover with the poorest sense
of timing, I can move away. Should I
be glad? Or shall I some time crave release
from this, become oppressive, liberty?
Those now about me, every age, are here
mostly in pairs or groups. It may be that
some states, events are best experienced
if shared. If not, they'll always seem to be,
like ghosts, ephemera, or passing dreams,
not truly undergone—encountering beauty,
say, in any of its forms, akin
to love, born even of love, and which gives life
to love. At such a time one may regret
perhaps, if fleetingly, the Villa d'Este
of one's youth, and where it did not lead.

...Isola Madre there.

It looks abandoned, lonely,
left. Is that a house?
Can one go there?

Another Borromeo
property, I've read.

Isola Madre, Lake Maggiore

A house, great wooded gardens,
not like here all formal.

Looks mysterious,
romantic, in this light.
Let's go tomorrow, Paul,
and see it. Oh, it was
so marvellous today.
I feel so happy, love...

The 'Mother Island', farther out, recedes
as now we sail, a cushion of green woods,
the single, long house bedded among trees,
remote, deserted-seeming in the dusk
after the populous bustle we have left.
Mysterious yes, and with a veiled allure.
Along the shores of Borromeo Bay
spring points of light. They glitter like the stars
that in a few hours more will mimic them
above, out of the dark, blue velvet sky.

When something's over, there's a haste to leave.
We swarm at Stresa, ant-like, from the boat,
disperse into the town, to cars left parked
below the trees, or to the waiting coaches
from far off. They scatter to the evening's,
night's activities, to spectacles
yet to be seen, or back again to where
they came from, and their lives, never to be
assembled as today loosely they've been,
by chance, in one place, with a common aim.

Some of us treasure beauties from the past,
for what and how they are, just in themselves,
for that past they in part encapsulate,
as symbols of the seeming better times
it is our wish, and need, to think, believe
may have been real. Especially we esteem,
the products of great craft—exuberance
of gardens, sumptuous palaces, creations
celebrating ceremony, flourish,
carnival, high flights of faith, the cresting
of the waves, the race on forceful tides

of purpose and triumphant hope.
We like, like to conserve, the boldness, challenge
of their statements, affirmations of
our upward-soaring spirit, self-regard.
Even most violent, radical upsets
of social systems have not ended them.
Reasons are found to justify and keep
Versailles, the palaces of Leningrad.
We prize the beautiful above most things,
strive to create it, as we have the means,
abilities and taste, destroy it too
sometimes, for that desire is part of us
no less to cast down what sustains, only
to build again as yet we must.

We've here seen beauty for an age that's past,
enjoyable by few, a very, very few
of that same age. What do we have in ours,
now, for the many, many more to whom
the comparable beauties are made free,
as within reach for being known and loved?
Those still to come may find, perhaps, preserve
and visit something of our time deemed worth
which may survive ourselves, although I cannot
now be certain what—if anything
at all survives for a posterity.

Over the bay the flecks of light begin
to merge, and mass into the glow of towns,
Pallanza of Verbania along
the point of Castagnola, and, across
the gap through which the main lake spreads towards
the north and east, Laveno and Cerro.

With the day cut off by the mountains' height,
air falls in chill reminder that high alps
circle almost near, that the snows which melt
are not as yet quite gone, in this late May.

Tomorrow, little doubt, the sun will shine
upon the lake again, all gold and blue.

Meeting Place

i

There's a landscape in my mind.
I don't know where it came from,
whether somewhere I have been,
or something dreamed.

It has upland fields and hedges
green and curved against the sky,
a solitary tree near where
two highways cross.

I'm travelling, and a lark sings
hidden in the spring blue.
The air is soft, and bridal crowns
are on the hawthorn.

ii

Marching as a soldier, twenty,
and an adulthood ago,
did I tramp here, or imagine
journeys in a landscape of my freedom.

Scentlike there drifts a feeling with it;
something is to happen, bringing joy,
the wished-for, meaningful involvement,
capture of hearts, success, or peace.

I've since been a long time travelling,
surely have passed by the imaged land,
perhaps not knowing this, or me,
leaving it yet to be encountered,
in its eternal springtime.

The Long Day Out

I left them early, at my dawn,
drove off to conquest in first light,
ground-ghosting mist of summer,
eyes on fleeing bounds.
All morning I've contended
on the hustling streets of Wraxham,
Battersby, and Millington,
in offices, exchange or market
thrust for gains and prospects,
hunted to win over
those who'll make it happen,
closed the deals that flaunted gilt.

The early hours were bright,
soon lost to search, crowns won,
and glories missed,
forgetfulness of much once loved,
the irreplaceables.
I had to know the blaze of summer,
high, the heat
and clamour of the day, though
trodden shadows chased.

The sun bedimmed by dust and straw,
homewards, with little triumphs, empty hands,
I've pulled in at The Upland View
on the road just out of Morlandridge,
surveyed what's got and spent.
It's well past noon, and unobserved
the may has gone.
The fragile porcelain of elder flowers
next will be fractured, shed,
the blush of dog-rose
blanched and blown like the surprise
of early snow.

The clouds swing up the sky and fray,
swirling, blacken to proclaim
the hounding storm. The leaves strain taut
like hair drawn from the bone
of ash and willow.

Cold
I must get back to Altonham this day
and find what may be left.

The little fish-shaped streaks of rain
appear on windows, swell and merge,
run down like tear-fall of regret.
I drive through evening and dissolving glass
as the light falters, leaden scene grows chill.
In front there is the tunnel of the way
beneath the vault of shrouding trees at Harrowholl,
down the dank deep and then
the stream to cross at Lethenbridge.

The road back's farther than I thought
when I set out it seems
a life ago.
I won't get there before it's dark—
must travel into night
and at another dawn I hope
be with them once again.

From A Dream

In a dream
I gather, scent
the greenest,
freshest growth
of earliest spring,
sorrel unpleating
down a bank,
blades of velvet grass,
close to my home,
and cry,
because I see
and scent the first
and freshest spring
at our own house,
hear from within
sounds of my mother,
family,
moving, being, there,
and think
one day I'll come
and they will not be here,
even in such a spring,
the house a ruin,
in some other way
not ours,
and now I cry
for joy
because these things
still are.

In the dream
perhaps I was
quite small.

Awake again,
I know
that that time
has long come
and been,
and that my eyes
are dry.

New Moon Through Glass

Up beyond my window
the hook of brightness,
blade-edge thin,
luminously slits
the evening blue.
As if cut, I wince,
drop eyes
to unsee,
curse inwardly.
I forget again,
have first looked on
the new moon through glass.

My mother had a superstition,
went outside.

I don't know what
was supposed to happen.
Did her care ensure
the calm years?
What troubles, sorrows
came from lapses?
Through glass
is about the only way
I see it.
Is the life I've had,
owing to month-linked
year-linked spells,
bad luck (I
wouldn't walk
under ladders)?

Old beliefs.
Can I say
if they touch me now?
But, among so much else,
these almost monthly twinges
bring her back.

The Quality Of Light

Made harsh by northern snow
this February glare
strikes sharply on my page,
hurting the eye.

                    Between
that table and the chair
at five on July afternoons
a parallelogram of gold
lay on the floor.
Past three in winter, fading day,
in sliding palest wash
along the wall
from chimneypiece to door,
moved only to recede.
September moon's cold sheen
of silver late at night
would fall
like summer sun
across my bed.

The quality of light
does not repeat itself,
determined by
each blend of climate, earth's
configurations, weather, sky.
And it was something different
there, at our house we've left
at last, my family's home,
mine too for long.
The views will be the same
from all the windows, range
of landscape framed inside my mind;
as then, interiors
which have enshelled our time
of being, with its hopes,
some happiness, and dread,
tranquilities, the sorrows,
death and change.
The light will still come through
the panes, and shed

its tones and patterns on the floors
and walls at the same hours
in the same way.

The people there now may
or may not wonder about us.
We do not come out at them
from the stones, or from
the aspects of the rooms
appointed differently.
These will not tell of us,
although some claim
that atmospheres remain
detectable.

Safer to feel that nothing
is left there that's part of us,
no lingering trace
or uncollected residue
to worry us
where we are now;
that all's upgathered, brought along
to the new place.

The wind round certain chimneys, eaves,
on autumn nights will sound the same,
and, in the Mays, the song of birds
will waken those too, living there.

A house has years so many more
than ours, or generations'
even. Strange to know
it will go on apart from us
until some time its far
remoter end will be,
in an eventual decay,
collapse, rebuilding, or
intended demolitions,
act of God, or man, or war.

Of us, what stays is less,
the least, a name
that battles time on stone

with luck a century or two,
at most, remembrance, or a fame
for what it may have been
that we could do.
How very small a part
is even this of all
that total essence
which a house enclosed,
the special light caressed.

This February is to go,
will peter out to March, and air
will soften, thaw, bring dreams
of loitering spring. Back there
the catkins soon will be on willow,
young fish in the streams.

The light will leave its legacy,
perhaps,
for those who've followed us.
We
have to find a new.

The Visits

At two p.m. each Saturday
my landlady set out
with basket and small garden tools
for the grave of her husband
long and early dead
('I've flowers growing for him there')
by town bus half an hour away.
Fiftyish, gentle and genteel
she lived by dress-making,
and let two pairs of rooms
to men in out-of-college years.
No children.

It was a ritual,
cheerful, festive almost. And
though even then I sensed
—what I know with feeling now—
that the weekly tending meant
communion and companionship
for which there was no substitute,
I found in it something sad
yet strange
prompting youth's inner smile.

Much later,
on a summer afternoon
I found that grave.
Her name too was on the stone—
there for some fifteen years.
Of the garden covering the plot
there was little trace
in the grasses' tall seed-spires
that shot to enmesh and overtop
the red, live requiescant
of a blossoming shrub rose.
A stretched, rank lupin
swayed in the errant breeze.
And high, high up
to a plane's drone
some thin cloud frayed
on July blue.

I have a grave of my own now
to visit from another land.
No more than once a year, until
that fails.
My tending is to place only
the cut blooms we bring there for them,
as much for ourselves, and, turned to go,
think of the few days' bright offerings,
the long shrinkage to dried remnants
I've found there on occasion
from last time,
and of the act, for love and conscience,
if beyond their knowing—all
that we can do.

New Beginnings

Far up, the cloud-packs race.
Moored in the bay a ship
chops at the waves.
It's March. Emotions rush
in witching swirls of dust
on the cliff path.
A paper bag, or rag,
strains from a bush.
Freed, it soars, zig-zags
directionless, then drops.

My occupation ends
this spring. Anchored
to place and times, those years
only in dreams I coursed
above the mast
with the driving cloud.

All of me now
can blow, be blown, about
this space of ours. The world
will, as we say, be mine.

Go, speed, with the gale
to follow what's been missed
or what is left to chase—
ideals recalled,
starts never made,
in the flying wind
where the last days crowd.

The Fledglings

The old men hunch on seats
by outside walls of churches,
in the town squares, in parks
where behind them
summer bushes drip.
At times
their heads turn, tilt.

The fledgling bird darts,
captures something, turns
its head to the side
as if satisfied,
perhaps exultant,
seeking praise.

They played together once.
For a time as youths
starting out, their lives touched.
They exchanged
arrogant ambitions,
dreams—nothing ordinary,
nothing dull for them—
and nurtured the while
unknowingly
the seeds of the possible.

Came a time when they could look
at friends' lives, sometimes even
see the whole cycle here completed,
from the outside think they could trace
a meaningful pattern.
In the same way tried
to see their own.

They acquiesced, lived their lives
as they could with what
they'd been given, watched
it happen.

Or were driven with a sense
of obligation
to protest the systems.

And what they did might not
have made much difference
except to them.

            One way
or another they've come
to here, to a new time
causing questioning,
bewilderment,
that demands turnings
of the head, searches, capture,
as the sun shines
or the leaves drip
and the bird flutters
from the bush,

through successive beginnings,
learnings how to cope.

Quiet Passage

When did you turn old?

When did the inner move
start working,
drift imperceptible

to age,
before that falter
on the stair,

the act or name
so unbelievably
forgotten

made another first aware
of what would stay,
increase to further change,

like the summer's end of growth,
a wheel in the wind or tide,
or the start of youth.

The Playing Field

From up on higher ground
the old man gazes down.
Distant, below
on the wide, extending field
the dog in chase looks round
to see
if it's companioned still.

Yes, the boy runs
drawn by the flying cloud
scenting
the mild soft air
of autumn or the spring,
and there,
about, beyond him
are the years
the world, oh everything
to keep him safe
and fill
his life with suns
of which the dreams now tell.

There is a hidden chain
which links these ends of time.
Will the young purpose hold,
or be cast out as wrong
and nothing's fantasy?
The chary, late-day steps,
the all, not quite enough,
that could be done,
the known continuance
to which we cling
too often are the endings
of that run.
And yet we long
sometimes, in the chill
of the veered wind,
for that warm dreamwhile
and the gold it spun.

'Shall I Have No Company...?'
Everyman

As the sun, hurtfully beautiful
in leaves, danced with shadow patches
on the ground, or under the bare
branches the earth rang, or snow,
blue-tinted in the shortest days,
softened footsteps and our words,
we've gone to where the lane meets
the highway when I had to leave,
and it was comfort that a someone
should be there, as long, as far,
as they could go
to the transporting off
to what I yet must face alone,
once school,
to be a soldier, into other
kinds of life.

Of those who came that way with me
now all are gone.
I leave alone to face
what new beginnings may be left,
without infusion of the strength
from knowledge of their presence,
thoughts, concern,
the parting glow
from love.

I have since learned to manage it,
a little coldly, emptily,
somehow.

But is there one,
for that last new beginning
which I'll fear to manage by myself
perhaps, who will be with me
in the summer-bright or darkening lane,
as far, as long, as they can go?

Of those I know now,
or will yet encounter,
I must wonder, who?

The Earlier Blights

Yesterday's gale has jack-knifed
the stems of many roses.
The blooms are living still.
But I must cut the broken,
hanging crowns.

They've flowered for me.
Now they are gone, like those
whose least expected deaths
I mourn,

who yet were dead to me before
as the friends they'd been,
from separation, mere defaults
in keeping track. The body's fall
just seals the truer death—
the dropping out
of one another's lives.

The storm has spared some heads.
They may keep opening
till December. To ourselves

we're flowering till the end,
however faded, or unseen,
or shrunken in the chill.

Tunings
To The Frequencies Of The Race

i

Feathers of rain brush
the window, globe, and merging
trickle down as tears.

ii

Late October born
I'm from the time of spirits
of the dead, blown leaves

and harvests gathered.
I begin with the dark world
of Demeter's night,

Persephone hail
with therefore a special joy
as my true springing.

iii

My birthday. Senders,
once, of cards have gone, more missed
than costliest gifts.

iv

I look out, recall
dead friends, the brighter prospects
lost, and wonder at

so small a measure
of regret, calm almost. This
helps us to get by.

v

King Lear wasn't mad
about the killing he knew.
Watch it on TV.

vi

Are the starved child's eyes
fear-widened more from hunger
or bewilderment?

vii

'Oh I'm so happy,
you can't guess.' Youth lives such joy
when the ride to all

its coursed aims looks clear.
Some feel of this lingers still.
Even in futile

ecstasy they cry,
but not believing, that it
can't be happening.

viii

Quick now, kids, to school.
Your Father's already left.
We're late. He *must* get

that promotion. Drop
them and then, will there be time
to make appointments

at the lawyer's and
the bank before the office?
Get ahead. Better

is more, we're told, and
more is—I shall *just* have time.
Rush, it's all rush, rush...

116

Home again at last.
Ah, that's poor Mr. Doneman
always looking out

(wave, wave). Time must now
lie heavy on his hands. But
it is all his own.

ix

I'm now of an age
when I must leave the old firm,
for so many years

a sheltering hedge
between me and neighbour self.
Now we're face to face.

In clearing my mind
of the clutter of a life
and work, from office

and attic, in my
emotional vacating,
this I'll throw away,

that keep in storage
till I want to bring it out
in another place.

x

For someone today
life will no more seem to breathe
indefinitely.

xi

Discarding, to save
only what is portable,
in this compelled time

of disassembling
the treasures of our days here,
it's hard to disperse

when inheritors
may not all be obvious
what we've collected,

to leave only thoughts
of the lost loved, and a kind
of wondering hope.

xii

Dying cheerfully
you met my frightened small talk.
Generous to me.

xiii

We live in war's shade,
light-cast shadow of our race.
Can a cloud dispel?

All past fear of war
did not deter. What of this
newer fear of fear?

xiv

Life is as it is
while it may last, with beauty,
art, the world of folk,

belief, work, nature,
love, ambition, to prepare
or unprepare you.

xv

A single black bird,
adrift, slips by as I draw
the curtains at five.

By this time in spring
there will be flocking, chatter
in lengthening light.

Talk, others on earth,
listen each to each, and drown
the stillness of death.

www.ingramcontent.com/pod-product-compliance
Lightning Source LLC
Chambersburg PA
CBHW060521030426
42337CB00015B/1966